# Discovering Religions
## Judaism

### Sue Penney

Heinemann

Heinemann Educational Publishers
Halley Court, Jordan Hill, Oxford OX2 8EJ

OXFORD PORTSMOUTH NH (USA) CHICAGO
MELBOURNE AUCKLAND IBADAN
GABORONE JOHANNESBURG BLANTYRE

First published 1987
Revised edition published 1995

99 98
10 9 8 7

**British Library Cataloguing in Publication Data**
A catalogue record for this book is available from the British Library

ISBN 0 435 30467 4

Designed and typeset by Visual Image
Illustrated by Gecko Limited. Adapted into colour by Visual Image
Produced by Mandarin Offset
Printed in Great Britain by Bath Press Colourbooks, Glasgow

**Acknowledgements**

Religious Studies consultant: W Owen Cole

Thanks are due to Rabbi Douglas Charing and Rabbi Arye Forta for reading and
advising on the manuscript.

The publishers would like to thank the following for permission to use photographs:
The Ancient Art and Architecture Collection p. 39; Werner Braun pp. 40 (top),
42 (top), 44; J Allan Cash Photo Library p. 32; Circa Photo Library pp. 12, 17; Bruce
Coleman Ltd p. 25; A H Edwards/Circa Photo Library p. 13; Robert Harding pp. 6, 38;
The Hutchinson Library p. 16; Jewish Education Bureau p. 8; The Jewish Museum
p. 23; B Key/Christine Osborne Pictures p. 37; Peter Osborne p. 40 (below);
Zev Radovan pp. 33, 34; Anat Rotem-Braun p. 21; Barrie Searle/Circa Photo Library
pp. 11, 27, 29, 31; Juliette Soester pp. 10, 14, 18 (below), 28, 42 (below), 45, 47;
The Weiner Library p. 36; Zefa pp. 7, 9, 15, 18 (top), 20, 22, 26, 46.

The publishers would like to thank Zefa for permission to reproduce
the cover photograph.

The publishers have made every effort to trace the copyright holders, but if they have
inadvertently overlooked any, they will be pleased to make the necessary
arrangements at the first opportunity.

296/PEN

# Contents

# *MAP:* where the main religions began

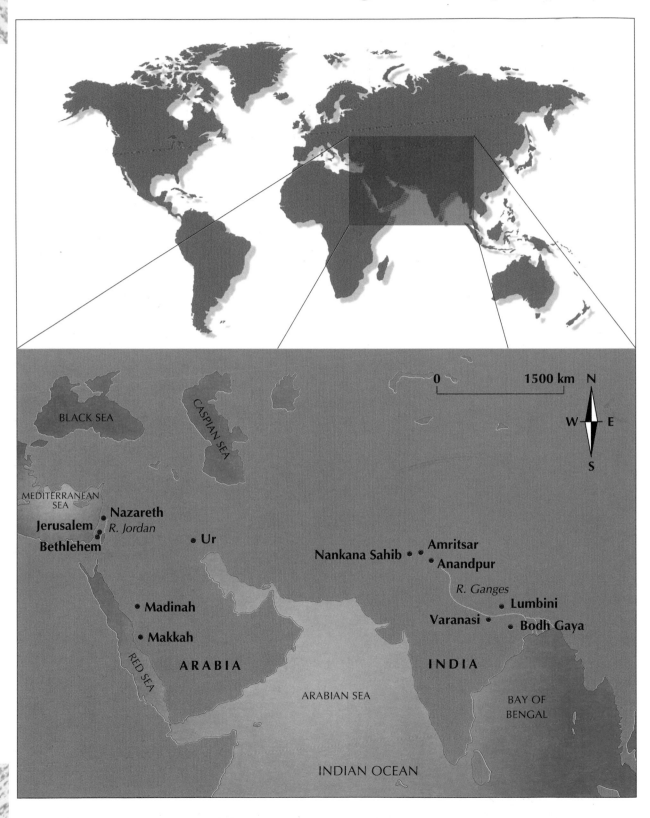

BLACK SEA

CASPIAN SEA

MEDITERRANEAN SEA

0               1500 km  N

W  E

S

**Nazareth**
**Jerusalem** *R. Jordan*
**Bethlehem**

• **Ur**

**Nankana Sahib** • • **Amritsar**
            • **Anandpur**

*R. Ganges*

• **Madinah**

                           • **Lumbini**
**Varanasi** •
               • **Bodh Gaya**

• **Makkah**

**A R A B I A**              **I N D I A**

RED SEA

ARABIAN SEA

BAY OF BENGAL

INDIAN OCEAN

# TIMECHART: when the main religions began

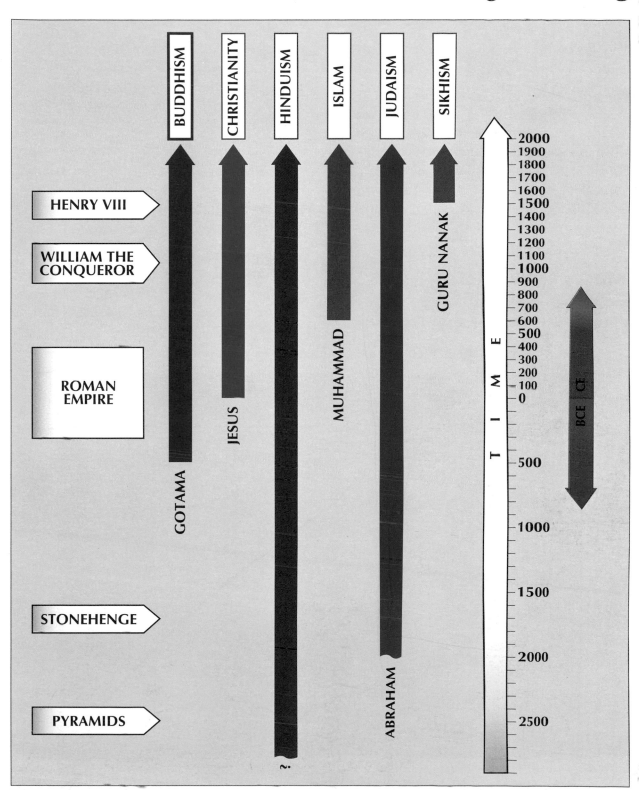

**Note about dating systems**

In this book dates are not called BC and AD which is the Christian dating system. The letters BCE and CE are used instead. BCE stands for 'Before the Common Era' and CE stands for 'Common Era'. BCE and CE can be used by people of all religions, Christians too. The year numbers are not changed.

# Introducing Judaism

This section tells you something about who Jews are.

The word 'Jew' can be used in two ways. It means someone who was born a Jew. It also means a Jew who follows the Jewish religion, which is called **Judaism**. Not everyone who was born Jewish chooses to keep to the religion. Some people who were not born Jewish choose to become followers of Judaism. In this book, 'Jew' means a follower of the religion of Judaism.

## What do Jews believe?

Jews believe that there is only one God, who is **eternal**. This means that he was never born and will never die. He is always present everywhere, and he knows everything. He made everything, including the world and everything in it. He cares about everything that he made and he listens when people pray to him.

When Jews pray to God, they call him **Adonai**. This means 'Lord'. Jews think that God's name is very important, so they use it with great respect. They never use it carelessly.

Jews do not believe that they are the only ones who know what God is like, but they do believe that Jews have a special relationship with God. They believe that God gave laws which they

*This modern sculpture of a menorah is in Jerusalem*

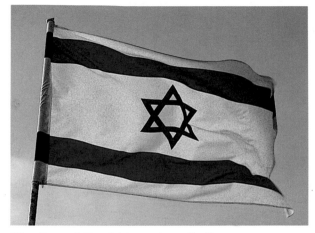

*The Star of David is on Israel's flag*

Temple was destroyed in 70 CE. It was the most important building in the Jewish religion.

The other symbol is a star with six points. This is called the Star of David, or sometimes the Shield of David. No one really knows where this symbol came from, but it has been used for hundreds of years. It is used as part of the flag of Israel, the country where many Jews live.

must obey. As long as they obey the laws, God will look after them. Their relationship with God is based on love. One of the prayers which Jews use most often shows how important this is. It says, 'You must love the Lord your God with all your heart, with all your mind and with all your strength'. This prayer is called the **Shema**.

## Jewish symbols

Jews use many **symbols** in their religion, but two are especially important. One is the **menorah**. It is a candlestick which has seven branches. It reminds Jews of the lamps which were used in the **Temple** in Jerusalem. The

## New words

**Adonai** name for God (means Lord)
**Eternal** lasting for ever
**Judaism** Jewish religion
**Menorah** seven-branched candlestick
**Shema** Jewish prayer
**Symbol** something which has a special meaning, or stands for something else
**Temple** most important place of Jewish worship (destroyed 70 CE)

## Test yourself

What do Jews call God when they pray to him?

What's the Shema?

What's a menorah?

What was the Temple?

## Things to do

1 Explain as carefully as you can the most important beliefs of the Jews.

2 Think of as many reasons as you can why Jews use God's name so carefully.

3 Some people have said that God is like a circle. Try to explain why. (**Clue:** Where does a circle begin or end?)

4 Symbols are often pictures which stand for something.
   a Draw the two Jewish symbols mentioned on this page, and for each one write a sentence explaining what it is.
   b Then think of two symbols which you use in everyday life. Draw them, and explain what they stand for.

# The synagogue

This section is about the special place where Jews worship, and the things you find there.

A **synagogue** is the building where Jews go to worship God. The building is also used as the place where Jewish children are taught about their religion, and learn **Hebrew**. Hebrew is the language in which the Jewish **Scriptures** are written, so it is important for Jews to understand it.

## Inside a synagogue

The most important thing in a synagogue is the **Ark**. This is a special cupboard, which is at the front of the main room. The **scrolls** are kept in the Ark. A scroll is like a book with one long page, which is unwound so that it can be read. The scrolls are very important, because the **Torah** is written on them.

*Inside a modern synagogue. (In this synagogue the women's section is upstairs)*

## Scrolls

A scroll is a long roll made of pieces of **parchment** stitched together. Parchment is made from animal skin which has been dried and smoothed so that it can be written on. The scroll has a wooden roller at each end, which the parchment is wound around. A scroll is about 60 metres long. Scrolls are written by hand, using special ink. The writing is in Hebrew. Scrolls are very important, and so they are looked after very carefully. The parchment is never touched with hands. When someone is reading from the scroll, a special pointer is used to follow the words.

Each scroll has a special cover which is used when it is put away in the Ark. The cover is called a **mantle**. It is usually made of silk or velvet. Mantles are often beautifully decorated with embroidery. Sometimes scrolls have other decorations, too. These are called the crown and bells. They help to remind people that the scrolls are important.

## Other important parts of the synagogue
### The ever-burning lamp

In front of the Ark is a lamp in which the flame never goes out. This helps to remind people that God is always present. It also reminds Jews of the lamp which was in the Temple.

*The Ark is at the front of the synagogue*

### The bimah

In the middle of the synagogue is a raised platform, which is called a **bimah**. The Torah is read from a table on this platform, and the person who is leading the service may stand there.

### The women's section

In most synagogues, men and women do not sit together. Women have a separate section of their own.

## New words

**Ark** cupboard which contains the scrolls
**Bimah** platform on which the reading desk stands
**Hebrew** Jewish language
**Mantle** cover for scrolls
**Parchment** writing surface made of animal skin
**Scriptures** holy books
**Scroll** roll of parchment on which the Torah is written
**Synagogue** Jewish place of worship
**Torah** Books of Teaching

## Test yourself

What's a synagogue?

What's Hebrew?

What's a scroll?

What's the bimah?

## Things to do

1 Use the information and the pictures on this page to help you write your own description of the Ark, the ever-burning light and the scrolls.

2 Scrolls are very important to Jews. Think of two reasons why they are looked after so carefully.

3 Why do you think that Jews use the symbol of a burning lamp to represent God?

4 Find out if it is possible to arrange a visit to a synagogue. If you cannot go to one, find out as much as you can from books or videos, and do a drawing or make a model showing what a synagogue is like.

# Worship in the synagogue

This section tells you about how Jews worship in the synagogue.

For Jews, worship means praying to God, thanking him for the things he has done and asking for his help in their lives. They believe that worshipping God is very important.

Jews do not believe that they can only worship God if they are in the synagogue. They worship him in other places too. But every **Shabbat**, the Jewish holy day, many Jews go to the synagogue because it is a special place to worship God. As they go into the synagogue,

Jews wash their hands. This is not because they are dirty, it is a symbol to make them fit for prayer. Then they say a prayer which thanks God for the fact that they can worship him.

A synagogue service includes readings from the Scriptures, prayers and singing of **psalms**. (A psalm is a sort of poem.) Usually there is a talk called a **sermon**. Some synagogue services include readings from the Torah, the Books of Teaching which are written on scrolls. The scrolls are carried carefully from the Ark to the bimah to be read, and back again after the reading is finished. For a full synagogue service to be held, ten men must be present. If there

*This boy is dressed for worship*

are not, the service will still be held, but not all of the prayers will be said.

## Special clothes

At services in the synagogue, men wear a **kippah**. A kippah is a skull cap, which is often beautifully embroidered. It is worn as a sign of respect for God – many Jewish men wear one all the time. At morning services, they also wear a **tallit**. A tallit is a prayer robe, usually made of silk or wool. It has a fringe and tassels at the ends.

In Orthodox synagogues (see pages 40–1), men wear two small black leather boxes with straps as well as the tallit and kippah. These boxes are called **tefillin**. They contain small pieces of parchment. The parchment has short quotations from the Scriptures written on it. One box is worn in the middle of the forehead. This reminds Jews that they must love God with all their mind. The other is worn on the arm, facing the heart. This reminds Jews to love God with all their heart.

*A tefillah (plural tefillin) with its contents*

## New words

**Kippah** skull cap
**Psalm** sort of poem, used like a hymn
**Sermon** special talk which teaches about religion
**Shabbat** Jewish holy day
**Tallit** prayer robe
**Tefillin** small leather boxes containing quotes from the Scriptures

## Test yourself

What's a psalm?

What's a kippah?

What's a tallit?

What are tefillin?

## Things to do

**1** Describe as carefully as you can the special clothes which a Jewish man wears for worship. Remember to include when he wears them.

**2** Why do you think Jews go to the synagogue if they believe they can worship God anywhere?

**3** Many synagogues and things used in worship are beautifully decorated. How many reasons can you think of why this is so?

**4** Choose two things which you would find being used in a synagogue. Draw them.

**5** Some of the Psalms are very well-known. Try to find out the words of some of them. (Looking in the Bible may help!)

# Jewish holy books

This section tells you about the Jewish holy books.

The complete Jewish Scriptures are called the **Tenakh**. They are divided into three sections.

- Torah  (The books of Teaching)
- Nevi'im  (The books of the Prophets)
- Ketuvim  (The 'writings')

Tenakh is a word made up of the first letters of these three names.

## The Torah

The Torah is the most important part of the Scriptures. It contains the books called Genesis, Exodus, Leviticus, Numbers and Deuteronomy. For reading in the synagogue, these books are written on scrolls.

The word 'Torah' means teaching. The Torah is a group of books which teach Jews what God is like, and how they should live. They include the stories about the creation of the world and about the first Jews. They also include the rules about worship, festivals and the right ways to live. Altogether, there are 613 rules in the Torah. They are about all parts of life. Some Jews follow them more strictly than others. Some Jews follow them very closely, because they believe that it means they are living their lives in the way that God wants.

Another collection of teaching about how to live is called the **Talmud**. It contains the teachings of **rabbis**, collected together over many years and written down in about 500 CE. The Talmud gives much more detail about the Laws in the Torah, and helps to explain them.

*Scrolls with their mantles and decorations*

*A scroll on the Bimah (notice the pointer, which is used when reading it)*

## Nevi'im

Nevi'im is a collection of books about the history of the Jewish people. It includes the teachings of the **prophets**. Jews believe that the prophets were men and women who had special powers given by God. This meant that they could tell people how God wanted them to live.

Some parts of Nevi'im are read in synagogue services. They are usually read from an ordinary book, not a scroll. Other parts of Nevi'im are not used in the synagogue, although Jews may read them at home.

## Ketuvim

Ketuvim means writings, and most of the books contain stories from Jewish history. The book of Ketuvim which is used most often is the Book of Psalms. A psalm is a special poem, rather like a hymn. Psalms are often used in synagogue services.

### New words

**Prophet** someone who tells people what God wants
**Rabbi** Jewish teacher
**Talmud** collected teachings of the rabbis
**Tenakh** Jewish Scriptures

### Test yourself

What's the Tenakh?

What's the Talmud?

What's a rabbi?

What's a prophet?

### Things to do

1 Draw a diagram to show how the Jewish Scriptures together make the Tenakh. You could use your own ideas, or fit the shapes here together to make a shape you recognize. When you have drawn it, describe what each part is about.

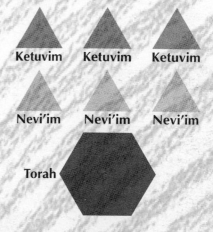

**The Tenakh**

2 Explain why many Jews feel they should keep the Laws of the Torah very carefully.

3 What sort of special powers do you think the prophets would need?

4 Make a small scroll, or draw a picture of an open scroll. Write on it something you have learned about what Jews believe.

# Shabbat

This section tells you about Shabbat, the Jewish day of rest and worship.

Shabbat is the Hebrew word for the Sabbath. It is the Jewish day of rest. It begins at sunset on Friday evening, and lasts until dusk on Saturday.

Shabbat is the oldest of the Jewish holidays. Jews remember the story in the book of Genesis about how God made the world. The story says that God worked for six days, and on the seventh day he rested. So Jews also rest on the seventh day of the week, which is Saturday.

Jews think that the Sabbath is very important. They believe that it is a special gift from God. It is a day of peace and rest. Jews look forward to the Sabbath all week. It is so special that it is sometimes called 'Queen Sabbath'.

## Celebrating Shabbat

During Friday, the house is tidied and the table set, so that everything is ready to welcome the Sabbath. The Sabbath begins at sunset on Friday evening. It is always the wife or mother in a Jewish family who begins the Sabbath celebrations. The first thing she does is light two candles. As she lights them, she says a prayer which asks God to bless the home.

There is always a service in the synagogue on a Friday evening. When the family return home, the father blesses the children, and reads from the Scriptures. Then they all sit down at the table for the Sabbath eve meal. This is the most important meal of the week, and every family tries to make it the best they can afford. It is a relaxed, happy meal when families can enjoy each other's company, and Jews look forward to it from one week to the next.

The table is always covered with a clean white cloth, and the meal begins when the father recites a blessing called the **kiddush** over a cup of wine. Sabbath hymns are sung as the family sits at the table. The Sabbath meal often includes special foods, and there are always two loaves of bread. This is called **challah bread**, which is specially baked for the Sabbath. A blessing is said over the bread before it is eaten.

*Lighting the Shabbat candles (notice the challah bread under its cover)*

On Sabbath morning, many Jews go to the service at the synagogue. To make the Sabbath different from any other day, and to show how important it is, Jews must rest completely, and not do any work. Cooking is forbidden, so all food is prepared the day before. Strict Jews observe the rules very carefully, and – for example – will not drive or go shopping. It makes Shabbat a day which they can enjoy by relaxing together without feeling that there are things to do.

The Sabbath ends on Saturday evening, when the father says another blessing called the **havdalah**. A special plaited candle is lit, and everyone smells a special box of spices. The pleasant smell of the spices spreads through the house. Jews hope that this is a symbol of the way the peace and quiet of Shabbat will be remembered all through the coming week. After the blessing, the havdalah candle is put out by dipping it in a cup of wine. Shabbat is over when three stars can be seen in the sky.

*The havdalah ceremony, with candle and spice box*

## New words

**Challah bread** special bread for the Sabbath

**Havdalah** blessing which ends the Sabbath

**Kiddush** blessing which begins the Sabbath

## Test yourself

What's Shabbat?

What's kiddush?

What's havdalah?

## Things to do

1 Do your own drawing of a havdalah candle or a spice box. Explain the part it plays in the Sabbath celebrations.

2 It is always a woman who begins the Sabbath celebrations. Why do you think this is so?

3 The Sabbath is a day when Jews can relax and enjoy being together. List as many advantages as you can for spending a day like this. What disadvantages might there be?

4 Write a paragraph explaining what Shabbat is, and why Jews think it is so important. Illustrate it with drawings if you wish.

5 Find out more of the story of how God made the world. It's in the Bible in the Book of Genesis, chapter 1.

# Rosh Hashanah and Yom Kippur

This section tells you about the important days at the time of the Jewish New Year.

## Rosh Hashanah

Rosh Hashanah is the Jewish New Year. Jews have their own calendar, so New Year is not on 1 January. It falls in late September or early October. Jewish years are also numbered in a different way. They are 3761 years ahead of the Gregorian calendar which is used in most countries. For example, the Jewish year 5756 began in autumn 1995, the year 5761 will begin in 2000, and so on.

Rosh Hashanah reminds the Jews how God made the world. It is also the beginning of the most solemn time of the year. This lasts for ten days, which are called the Days of Returning. In these ten days, Jews think about the things they have done wrong in the past year. They make promises to themselves and to God that they will do better in the future.

The night before Rosh Hashanah, Jews have a meal at home. A special part of the meal is eating apples dipped in honey. This is a way of saying that everyone wishes that the year which is beginning will be sweet and pleasant.

A special synagogue service is held at Rosh Hashanah. The **shofar** is blown. A shofar is a ram's horn, hollowed out so that notes can be played on it. The notes it plays sound very solemn. They remind the people that God is very powerful, and they must listen to him.

## Yom Kippur

Yom Kippur comes at the end of the Days of Returning. It is the Day of **Atonement**, which is the most solemn day of the year. Atonement means making up for something you have done wrong. It is a day when Jews pray to God to forgive them for the things they have done wrong.

*Eating apples and honey*

*Blowing the shofar*

At Yom Kippur, Jews **fast** for 25 hours. (This means they go without any food or drink.) They spend a lot of the day at the synagogue. They believe that if they are really sorry for the wrong things they have done God will forgive them. As well as praying for forgiveness, Yom Kippur is a day for remembering how kind God is, and how much he loves them. In the synagogue, the Ark and the reading desk are covered in white cloths, and the people leading the service wear white, too. This is a symbol to show that God has taken away the sins of the people who are sorry for what they have done wrong.

At the end of the service, the shofar is blown again. Its meaning is different from when it was blown at Rosh Hashanah. This time it reminds people that they must remember all the good things they have promised to do, and live good lives throughout the coming year.

## New words

**Atonement** making up for something you have done wrong
**Fast** go without food and drink, often for religious reasons
**Shofar** ram's horn instrument

## Test yourself

What's Rosh Hashanah?

What's Yom Kippur?

What's atonement?

What's a shofar?

## Things to do

**1** Using the information and the pictures on these pages, how many symbols can you find which Jews use at Rosh Hashanah and Yom Kippur? Explain what each symbol means.

**2** Do you think having a special time to think about the way you behave is a good idea? Why?

**3** Fasting is often part of serious religious festivals. Why do you think this is so?

**4** Write a poem or draw a picture to show what being sorry means to you.

**5** Promises to do better are often called New Year's Resolutions. Think of five resolutions it would be a good idea for you to make. Work in pairs to discuss your ideas.

# Sukkot

This section tells you about Sukkot, the Feast of **Tabernacles**.

Tabernacle is an old word which means a sort of hut. The Hebrew word for this hut is **sukkah** (plural sukkot). The Feast of Tabernacles is the second festival of the Jewish year. In Hebrew it is called Sukkot. The festival lasts a week. Jews build a sukkah in the garden, and live in it for the week.

The Feast of Tabernacles celebrates two things.

- It recalls how the Jews in olden days used to take offerings of fruit to the Temple.

- It recalls how the Jews were once travelling in the desert and lived in tabernacles.

The most important part of the sukkah is the roof. This is made of branches, and has fruit

*A sukkah*

hung from it. It is built so that the sky can be seen through it. This is a reminder of the time in Jewish history when Jews were travelling in the desert with no proper home.

At the special synagogue service, everyone holds branches of certain trees – these are

*Carrying the lulav and citron*

called the 'lulav'. The trees are palm, willow and myrtle. The people hold the branches in their right hands. In their left hands they each hold a citron. A citron is a yellow fruit rather like a lemon. During the service, the people walk around the synagogue carrying these things. They also wave the branches. They are waved in all directions to show that God rules all the universe.

Each of the things they carry has a meaning. A sign or object that has a special meaning is called a symbol. The palm symbolizes the spine. The willow symbolizes the lips. The myrtle symbolizes the eyes. The citron symbolizes the heart. Joining them together reminds Jews that God must be worshipped with every part of them.

## Simchat Torah

The day after the end of the Feast of Tabernacles is called Simchat Torah. This means the Rejoicing of the Torah. The books of the Torah are Genesis, Exodus, Leviticus, Numbers and Deuteronomy. They are very important for Jews. Parts of the books are read every week in services in the synagogue. During the year, the five books are read all through. At Simchat Torah, there is a special ceremony when the last part of the book of Deuteronomy is read, followed by the first part of the book of Genesis. Jews believe that the books show the way God wants them to live, so reading them like this is a way of showing that they should never stop following what God wants.

Simchat Torah is a very happy day. All the scrolls are taken out of the Ark and carried round the synagogue with the people dancing, singing and clapping after them. To celebrate the festival, children in the synagogue are given bags of sweets and fruit.

## New words

**Sukkah** Hebrew word for tabernacle
**Tabernacle** sort of hut

## Test yourself

What's a tabernacle?

What does waving the branches show?

What is read at Simchat Torah?

## Things to do

1 Describe what a sukkah is like. When is it built? What must it include? What do you think it is like to live in?

2 How do Jews remind themselves of their history during Sukkot?

3 Explain why it is important for Jews that they read the last part and the first part of the Torah on the same day.

4 Find out what palm, willow and myrtle leaves look like. Then use drawings to help you explain why they are used as symbols for the spine, lips and eyes.

# Hanukkah

This section tells you about the festival of Hanukkah.

Hanukkah is a winter festival. It usually falls in December, and it lasts for eight days. It is sometimes called the 'Festival of Lights'.

## The story of Hanukkah

Hanukkah reminds the Jews of events that happened over two thousand years ago. It celebrates the bravery of a small group of Jews who were led by a man called Judah. His nickname was 'the hammer'. In Hebrew, hammer is 'maccabee' so he is called Judah the Maccabee.

*Lighting the hanukiah*

Judah was the leader of a small group of men who were fighting for what they believed. Their country had been taken over by an enemy. The new ruler was called Antiochus. He would not let the Jews worship their own God. He said that they had to worship him! The Jews knew that Antiochus was only a man, and it would be wrong to worship him.

Judah and his small group of friends fought against the cruel emperor Antiochus for three years. At last they managed to beat his army in a battle. The battle was important, because it meant that they had captured Jerusalem. Jerusalem is a very important city for the Jews. The Temple was in Jerusalem, and the Temple was the most important building in the Jewish religion. Antiochus had tried to spoil the Temple, so that Jews could not use it. He had ordered that a pig should be killed on the altar, one of the most important parts of the Temple. This made the Temple unclean – far worse than just dirty. It could not be used to worship God again until it had been specially cleaned and made holy again.

After Judah had captured Jerusalem, one of the first things he did was give orders that the Temple should be made fit to worship God again. When the Temple was ready, the menorah was lit. This was the Temple lamp, which had seven branches. The menorah was supposed to burn all the time, but Antiochus had let it go out. When it was re-lit, Judah's men discovered that it only had enough oil in it to burn for one night. They went to fetch more, but the oil was special, and it took eight days to get it. When the soldiers got back, the lamp was still alight. The people said that this was a **miracle**. God had made the lamp burn even though it did not have enough oil. This showed that he was pleased that the Temple had been made fit to worship him again.

*Playing the dreidle game*

## Celebrating Hanukkah

When they celebrate the festival today, Jews use a special candlestick in their homes. It is called a **hanukiah**. It is a candlestick with eight branches and an extra holder for the 'servant candle' which is used to light all the others. One candle is lit on the first night of the festival, two on the second night, and so on. Each one is lit using the ninth candle. Before each candle is lit, special prayers are said. By the end of the festival, all nine candles are burning. Some Jews burn olive oil instead of candles, so that it is more like the miracle in the Temple.

Hanukkah is a very happy festival, especially for children. They go to parties and give each other presents. There is a special game which children play at Hanukkah using a four-sided top called a **dreidle**. On each side of the dreidle there is a Hebrew letter. The letters are the first letters of the Hebrew words which say 'A great miracle happened here'.

## Test yourself

Who was Judah?

Who was Antiochus?

What's a hanukiah?

## Things to do

**1** Look at the picture which shows the lighting of the hanukiah. Describe carefully what the hanukiah is like, and how it is used.

**2** Why do you think Judah was called 'the hammer'?

**3** Explain why what Antiochus had done to the Temple was so important to the Jews. How do you think they felt?

**4** Working in small groups, imagine you are a news reporter in Jerusalem on the day it is captured by Judah the Maccabee. Work out your report for the evening news. (Think about things like how the people are feeling, what work has to be done, what happened to the armies.)

# Purim

This section tells you about the festival of Purim.

Purim is a very exciting festival, especially for children. It takes place in February or March. Purim tells the story of a good queen and a bad man. The story is in the Jewish Scriptures and in the Bible. It is called the Book of Esther.

## The story of Purim

Esther was the name of the good queen. The bad man was called Haman. They lived a long time ago in a country called Persia. Haman was the King's Chief Minister in the government. He had quarrelled with a Jew who refused to bow as Haman passed. Bowing is a sign of worship, and Jews believe that it is wrong to worship anyone except God. Haman disliked the Jews, and because he was so angry he made a plan to kill all the Jews in Persia. To do this, he had to get the king to order the killings. Haman went to the king and told lies about the Jews. The king agreed that all Jews in the country should be killed. Haman could not make up his mind on which day the killings should be carried out, so he decided to draw lots. Purim is a word for 'lots', and this gives the festival its name.

Queen Esther heard about this. Although the king did not know it, she was Jewish. She decided that the Jews must be saved. The only way this could happen was if she could persuade her husband – the king – to change

*A play for Purim*

*This scroll of the Book of Esther is in the Jewish Museum in London*

his mind. This was a dangerous thing to try to do – she was only supposed to go to see the king when he sent for her! She was very brave. She invited the king and Haman to a feast. During the meal she told her husband the real reason why Haman wanted to kill all the Jews. The king was very angry. He ordered that Haman should be killed, and all the Jews were saved.

## Celebrating Purim

At the Festival of Purim, the story of how all this happened is read out in the synagogue. Every time the children hear the name of Haman, they make as much noise as they possibly can. They hiss and stamp their feet. They use special rattles (called **greggors**) and whistles. The idea is to make so much noise that Haman's name cannot be heard at all.

At Purim, children often go to fancy dress parties. Sometimes they put on special plays at school or in the synagogue to show the story. In Israel there are plays and carnivals in the streets. Purim is also a time when Jews give money to charity, and give gifts of food to each other. This makes sure that even poor people can celebrate the festival with a special meal.

## New word

**Greggor** rattle used by children at Purim

## Test yourself

Who was Esther?

Who was Haman?

What did Haman want to do?

Why did Haman want to get rid of the Jews?

## Things to do

1 **a** What can you tell about the power of the king from this story?
  **b** Do you think that Haman deserved what happened to him?

2 Why do you think Jews try to drown out the name of Haman in the readings?

3 Write the entry which Queen Esther might have made in her diary the night she heard about Haman's plot.

4 The book of Esther does not mention God, but Jews believe that the story shows God at work. Try to explain how this is so.

5 Working in groups, make up a play or a mime to show the story of Purim.

# Pesach

This section tells you about the story of Pesach, the Feast of Passover.

Passover is the most important Jewish festival. It celebrates something that happened nearly 4000 years ago. In those days, the Jews were living in Egypt. The king of Egypt was called the **Pharaoh**. The Pharaoh had made the Jews slaves. Their lives were very difficult. They had to work very hard, and were very badly treated. They had to build enormous storehouses for the Pharaoh. He had special slave-drivers to make them work hard. If they did not work fast enough – or if the slave-drivers felt like it – they were beaten with whips.

One of the Jews was a man called Moses. God spoke to Moses, telling him that he was to rescue the Jews. He went to the Pharaoh and said, 'Let my people go!' The Pharaoh refused, but then a series of disasters happened in Egypt. They are called **plagues**. Everyone believed that these plagues had been sent by God. Flies, frogs, locusts, cows dying ... altogether there were ten plagues. Each time there was a plague, the Pharaoh said that the Jews could go. As soon as the plague ended, he changed his mind and said that they must stay. The last plague was the most terrible. The eldest son in each Egyptian family died. God warned Moses that this would happen. He told Moses to tell the Jews to put lambs' blood on the doorposts of the Jewish houses. Then the Jewish boys would not die.

*The ten plagues*

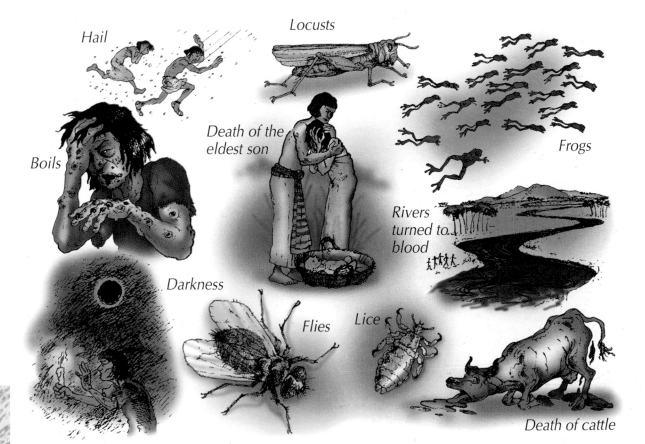

*Hail*

*Locusts*

*Boils*

*Death of the eldest son*

*Frogs*

*Rivers turned to blood*

*Darkness*

*Flies*

*Lice*

*Death of cattle*

The Pharaoh was so upset by the death of the boys that he said the Jews really could go. They prepared to leave as quickly as they could. They needed food for the journey, but there was no time to wait for the yeast to rise in the bread which they made. It was baked as it was. Although he had said they could leave, the Pharaoh changed his mind again. He sent his army after the Jews to bring them back. They were saved because of the water in the Sea of Reeds. It parted to allow them to cross. As soon as the Egyptian army tried to follow them, the sea flooded back and the Egyptians were drowned.

Passover reminds the Jews of three things.

- God is good – he helped his people.

- Death 'passed over' the houses of the Jews.

- The Jews passed over the Sea of Reeds when they were leaving Egypt.

*One of the plagues was a swarm of locusts*

## New words

**Pharaoh** king of Egypt

**Plague** disaster sent by God

## Test yourself

Who was the Pharaoh?

Who asked the Pharaoh to let the Jews go?

What's a plague?

## Things to do

1 Using the pictures and the information on these pages to help you, describe what you think it must have been like when the plagues were happening in Egypt.

2 Why do you think that the Pharaoh changed his mind whenever the plagues finished?

3 Explain the reasons why this festival is called 'Passover'.

4 Find out more about why the Jews were slaves in Egypt. (The section on Moses, on pages 34–5, will help.)

5 Working in small groups, discuss what you think it would feel like to be a slave. Write a poem or draw a picture to show your ideas.

# Celebrating Pesach

This section tells you how Jews celebrate Pesach, the Feast of Passover.

Passover takes place in late spring. Before the festival begins, the house is cleaned. Any **leaven** is removed. Leaven is anything like baking powder or yeast which makes dough rise. This is a reminder that when the Jews were leaving Egypt there was no time for the bread to rise. On the night before the festival begins, the house is searched. Any tiny piece or crumb of leaven is swept up with a feather and burned. Nothing which contains leaven is eaten during the festival.

## The Seder

The main part of the Passover celebration is a meal. This is called the **Seder**. The Seder meal follows a special 'order' which is written down in a book called the **Hagadah**. The Hagadah tells the story of the slavery and how the Jews left Egypt. The story is told as the meal is eaten. The youngest child present at the meal asks four questions. The questions are answered as the family read the story. In the answers to the questions, the person leading the meal talks about the things on the Seder plate. This is a special plate divided into five sections. Each

section contains a special food. The foods are symbols which remind the Jews of the slavery and how they left Egypt.

## Special foods for the Seder

- Shank bone – not eaten, but a reminder of the lamb which was killed so its blood could be put on the doorposts.

- Egg – hard-boiled, then roasted in a flame. A reminder of the animals which used to be **sacrificed** in the Temple, and a symbol of new life.

- Green vegetable – usually parsley or lettuce. A symbol of the way God cared for the Jews when they were travelling in the desert.

- Bitter herbs – usually horse-radish. A symbol of the bitterness of slavery.

- Charoset – a sweet mixture of apples, nuts, spices and wine. A reminder of the 'cement' used by the slaves when they were building, and a symbol of the sweetness of freedom.

There are three other important things on the table.

*The Seder meal*

*The Seder plate with matzot (plural of matzah)*

- A bowl of salt water, which is a symbol of the tears of the slaves. The parsley or lettuce is dipped in this.

- A glass of wine for each person. Wine is drunk four times during the meal. This is a reminder of the four promises which God made to Moses.

- **Matzot**, which are flat 'cakes' of unleavened bread. These are a reminder of the bread which did not rise.

Not everything eaten at Passover has a meaning. The Seder also includes a 'proper' meal. At the end of the Seder, the family stay at the table and sing songs. Many have repeated words or phrases, which even very young children can enjoy joining in.

Passover reminds Jews of their history, and of how Jews have suffered more recently. It helps them to look forward to a time of peace and joy. The last words of the Seder are:

*Next year in Jerusalem,*
*Next year may all be free.*

## New words

**Hagadah** book in which the Seder is written
**Leaven** yeast, baking powder, etc.
**Matzot** unleavened bread
**Seder** special Passover meal
**Sacrifice** offering made to a god

## Test yourself

What's the Seder?

What story does the Hagadah tell?

What are matzot?

## Things to do

1 Describe what happens at a Passover meal. Make sure you include the reasons for each of the customs.

2 Choose three of the special foods eaten at Passover, and explain why they are symbols.

3 Jews think their history is very important. How many ways can you think of in which Passover shows this?

4 If possible, prepare some or all of a Passover meal as a class. If this is not possible, work in groups to make a wall chart showing the story of Passover and how Jews celebrate it.

# Shavuot

This section tells you about Shavuot, the Feast of Pentecost.

The Feast of Pentecost is held seven weeks after the Feast of Passover. This is why it is sometimes called the Feast of Weeks. In Hebrew its name is Shavuot. It celebrates the Jews' belief that God gave the Ten Commandments to Moses.

Before the festival begins, the synagogue is decorated with fruit and flowers. This is often done by the children. It reminds people of how Mount Sinai bloomed with flowers when God came down to give the Torah to Moses.

## Celebrating Shavuot

The festival begins with a service in the synagogue. This includes the reading from the Scriptures about how God gave the Ten Commandments to Moses. The Ten Commandments are a set of rules about how to live. Jews believe that they were given to Moses when the Jews were travelling in the desert after they had left Egypt. Jews believe that this is the most important thing that has ever happened to human beings, because it was God telling people how he wanted them to live.

*Synagogues are decorated for Shavuot*

Many of the Ten Commandments are quite long, but the rules they give can be summed up like this.

1  I am the Lord your God. You must not have any other gods but me.

2  You must not make any **idols** to worship.

3  You must not use God's name carelessly.

4  Remember to keep the Sabbath day holy.

5  Respect your father and your mother.

6  You must not murder.

7  You must not commit **adultery**.

8  You must not steal.

9  You must not tell lies about other people.

10  You must not **covet**.

After the synagogue service, there is a festival meal at home. Part of the meal is two special loaves of bread. They are decorated with a ladder pattern. This reminds Jews of how Moses climbed Mount Sinai to talk to God and be given the Ten Commandments.

*Ladder bread*

## New words

**Adultery** sexual relationship outside marriage
**Covet** be jealous of what someone else owns
**Idol** false god (often a statue)

## Test yourself

What is Shavuot?

What did God give Moses?

What's an idol?

## Things to do

1  Use the photograph to help you describe how Jews decorate the synagogue for Shavuot. What do they use and why?

2  Explain why Jews think that the giving of the Torah was so important.

3  What sort of idols do you think people worship today?

4  Make sure you understand what each of the Ten Commandments means. Write them out in your own words. How important do you think they are today?

# Jewish history

This section tells you something about Jewish history.

Jewish history began about 4000 years ago in the part of the world that today we call the Middle East. No one person ever 'began' Judaism. The beliefs that became the Jewish faith came about gradually. However, some people were important in making it happen.

One of the most important men was called Abraham (see pages 32–3). He was the first to believe that there was only one God. He left his home and went on a long journey, because he believed that was what God wanted him to do. God showed him the way to a new country called Canaan. God promised Abraham that one day his descendants would possess this country. This is the reason it is sometimes called the Promised Land.

After Abraham, the next great leader was a man called Moses (see pages 34–5). He lived about 500 years after Abraham. When Moses

was alive, the Jews were slaves in Egypt. Moses became their leader and rescued them from slavery. These are the events which are remembered at Passover. After they left Egypt, the Jews lived in the desert for about 40 years. Then they settled back in Canaan again.

Jews lived around that area for hundreds of years, although the country's name and its borders changed many times. For most of the time, they were ruled by kings. One of the most famous kings was David. He lived about 3000 years ago. When David became king the country was very small and very poor, and the government was badly organized. David changed all that. He ruled well, and the country became rich and respected.

Other people who played an important part in the history of the country were not part of the government. They were called prophets. A prophet is someone who tells people what God wants. Sometimes they told kings too! Some of the prophets were important people in the country. Others were ordinary men and

*Historical map of the Middle East*

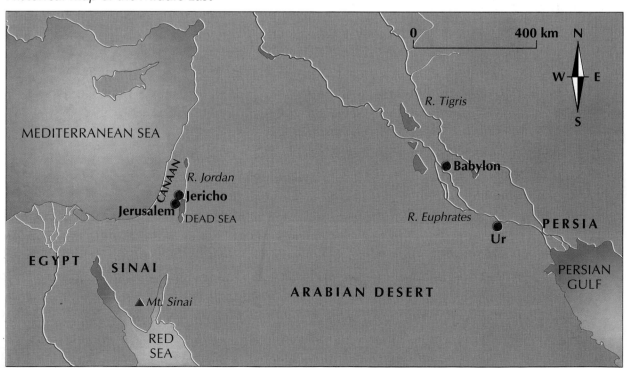

*Jews today come from all parts of the world (this boy comes from Ethiopia)*

about 2600 years ago. He was sure that God wanted him to warn the people that the way they were behaving was wrong. He told them that it would lead to the country being destroyed by an enemy. The people did not like being told this, and Jeremiah was very unpopular. He was put in prison, and people tried to kill him. Even though he did not want to carry on preaching, he felt he had to. He said that God's message was like 'a fire burning inside him'. His words came true in 598 BCE when Jerusalem was taken over by invaders from a place called Babylon.

During their history, the Jews' country has been taken over several times. Other nations ruled over them. Sometimes Jews were taken away from their own land and made to live in their enemy's country. Other Jews left by choice, because they did not want to live being ruled over by their enemies. They went to find a new life somewhere else. This is one of the reasons why today there are Jews all over the world.

women. They all felt that God was telling them what to do and say.

One of the most important prophets was a man called Jeremiah. He lived in Jerusalem

## Test yourself

What did Abraham believe?

What happened to the country when David was king?

What did all the prophets believe?

## Things to do

**1** Explain why the land which used to be called Canaan is very important to Jews.

**2** Why do you think rulers sometimes took Jews away from their own country?

**3** Try to find out more about King David. Write a short article, explaining why he was such an important king. (You will find information in books about Israel's history, and in the Bible – from I Samuel chapter 17 to I Kings chapter 2.)

**4** The prophets often told people about the things that were wrong in the life of the country. If you were a prophet in Britain today, what things do you think you would talk about? Discuss this in groups, then write about your ideas.

# Abraham

This section tells you about the first founder of Judaism.

Judaism did not suddenly 'begin'. It developed gradually, and came about through many different people. One of the first and most important of these people was a man called Abraham. He is often called one of the 'fathers' of Judaism.

Abraham lived about 4000 years ago in a town called Ur. Ur was in the part of the world that today we call Iraq. It was a very splendid city. It had gardens and tall buildings. Abraham was rich and respected. He and his wife Sarah had servants and lots of sheep and camels. In those days, the number of animals someone owned showed how rich they were.

The people of Ur worshipped many gods. There were gods of the sun, the moon and the stars. Their worship included many things which Abraham began to see were wrong. For example, they were worshipped with human sacrifices. This means that people were killed so that their life could be an offering to the gods. Abraham began to think that there was one God who ruled everything. He was more important than all the other gods. Gradually, Abraham became more and more sure about this 'true' God. He also became sure that God did not want to be worshipped in evil ways.

Abraham felt that God was telling him to leave Ur and travel to another country. He and his family set out. They did not know where they were going, but they believed that God would show them the way to go. In those days, people often moved around from place to place, because they needed to search for water for their animals. This is called being a **nomad**. Abraham's journey was different, because he felt he was being guided by God.

As they travelled, Abraham felt that he was getting to know more about his God. He felt that a special relationship was beginning. Jews

*Moon gods in Ur were worshipped in ziggurats like this*

32

*These nomads still live in much the same way as Abraham did*

believe that God promised Abraham that he would become the father of a great nation. All his children and their children for ever would have this same special relationship with God.

## New word

**Nomad** person with no fixed home

## Test yourself

What title do Jews give Abraham?

Where did Abraham live?

What's a nomad?

## Things to do

**1** How many reasons can you think of why Abraham left the town of Ur?

**2** Why do you think the people of Ur worshipped their gods with human sacrifices?

**3** Jews often call Abraham 'Father Abraham'. Try to explain why they do this.

**4** Imagine you are part of Abraham's family setting out with him from Ur. Write a story explaining how you feel and what you think is going to happen.

**5** Explain as carefully as you can the promise which Jews believe God made to Abraham.

# Moses

This section tells you about Moses.

Moses was the second great leader of the Jews. He lived at a very difficult time in Jewish history. For many years, the Jews had been slaves in Egypt. They were treated with great cruelty by their Egyptian masters. The Egyptians were afraid that the Jews might try to take over the country, so they decided that they must get rid of all Jews in Egypt. As part of this, they ordered that all baby boys should be killed at birth. Moses was not killed, because his mother hid him in a basket by the side of the river. He was found by the Pharaoh's daughter. She took him back to the palace and brought him up as if he were her own son.

When Moses grew up, he saw that the Jews were being very badly treated. One day he lost his temper and killed a slave-driver who had beaten a Jew to death. Then he had to leave Egypt, or he too would have been killed. He stayed away for several years, but gradually he became sure that God had work for him to do. God spoke to him, telling him to go back and get the Jews freed from slavery. At first he tried to make excuses to God about not going back, but at last he did. The Pharaoh did not want to let the Jews go, but a series of disasters (plagues) happened in Egypt. Moses told the Pharaoh that these plagues were sent by God, and at last the Pharaoh agreed to free the Jews.

The Jews' troubles were not over even after they had left Egypt. They spent the next 40 years wandering from place to place. They were nomads. These are called the years in the **wilderness**. A wilderness is like a desert where not very much grows. Eventually they found their way to the country called Canaan, and this became their home.

During the years when they were wandering, Moses was the Jews' leader. Jews believe that whilst they were in the wilderness, God gave Moses the Torah, the Teaching which Jews follow. This Teaching is very important for Jews, because it is part of their agreement with God. This agreement is a very serious one. It is called the **Covenant**. God promised that the Jews

*This Egyptian painting shows the Jews as slaves*

*The life of Moses*

## Test yourself

What work did God have for Moses?

What were the plagues?

What did God give Moses in the wilderness?

What was God's second promise?

## Things to do

**1** Make up a conversation which might have taken place between Moses and the Pharaoh. What arguments might Moses use to persuade the Pharaoh to let the Jews leave?

**2** Explain what the Covenant is, and why it is important to Jews.

**3** Find out as much as you can about the life of Moses. The information on pages 24–5 and 30–31 will help. There will be more information in your school or local library. Work in groups, and put together a wall display of your work.

**4** What do you think makes a good leader? Think of as many examples as you can of people in recent years who you think have been good leaders. Give reasons for your choice.

would be his 'Chosen People'. This does not mean that they would be his favourites. It means that they were chosen to be given extra responsibilities. God would look after them but, in return, the Jews must obey the laws which God gave.

In Jewish history, this is remembered as God's second promise to the Jews. The first promise was to Abraham – God promised that Abraham would be the father of a great nation. The second promise was to Moses – God would take special care of the Jews, if they obeyed his laws.

# Persecution

This section tells you about how Jews have been punished for their faith.

**Persecution** means being punished for what you believe. Jews have been among the most persecuted people in history. No one has ever been able to explain why this is so. The most likely reason is that Jews have been misunderstood. For example, Jews believe that they are God's 'chosen people'. Sometimes non-Jews have thought that this means that Jews feel they are better than other people.

Keeping their own religion and customs is very important for Jews. This has been the only way that their religion has survived. Sometimes this was seen by other people as being dangerous or threatening. It meant that Jews were 'different', and people are often afraid of what they do not understand. Sometimes, customs were really misunderstood. In other cases, they were deliberately 'twisted' so that Jews could be accused of things they had not done. In the Middle Ages, Jews were often persecuted by **Christians** who blamed them for killing Jesus. This was one reason why Jews were not allowed even to live in England for over 500 years.

The most serious persecution of Jews took place in the 1930s and '40s, when the Nazis were in power in Germany. Their leader was Adolf Hitler, and he hated the Jews. Dislike because of race or religion is called **prejudice**. Hitler was totally prejudiced against Jews, and he set out to destroy them completely. Little by little, all the Jews' rights were taken away. First, all Jews had to register at a local office. Then they were not allowed to go outside unless they were wearing a badge with the Star of David on it, so that they could be recognized in the street. No one was allowed to buy things from Jewish shops. Jews were not allowed to own cars or use buses or trains. Children were not allowed to go to school. Jews were not allowed to be

*Jews in Nazi Germany had to wear a Star of David badge*

outside after 9 p.m. ... The list went on and on. Then the Nazis introduced what they called the 'final solution to the Jewish problem'. Special camps were organized, and Jews were rounded up like animals. Some were killed at once. Others were starved, not allowed enough clothes, and had their hair shaved off. Torture was common, and every day thousands were sent to the gas chambers.

By the end of World War II, one in every three Jews in the world had been killed. Six million Jews, one and a half million of them children, were dead. This is too many to imagine, but think of it as equal to one in nine people in the British Isles today.

It is important to ask how this could happen. Most of the people who mistreated the Jews were more or less 'normal'. They acted as they did because Hitler managed to persuade them that Jews were not human. He said they were animals, who were responsible for all the many problems which Germany had at that time. This is called making someone a **scapegoat** – blaming them for something which is not their fault. Many people in Germany were ready to make the Jews scapegoats for all their problems, and so the Jews were persecuted.

The awful suffering which they have gone through helps to explain why many Jews today are very aware of their 'Jewishness'. It also explains why family life is so important.

> 'First they came for the Jews
> and I did not speak out –
> because I was not a Jew.
> Then they came for the communists
> and I did not speak out –
> because I was not a communist.
> Then they came for the trade
> unionists and I did not speak out –
> because I was not a trade unionist.
>
> Then they came for me –
> and there was no one left
> to speak out for me.'

*These words were written by Pastor Niemoller, a victim of the Nazis*

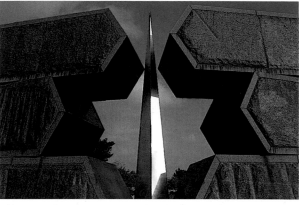

*This sculpture is part of the memorial at Yad Vashem to Jews killed by the Nazis*

## New words

**Christian** follower of Jesus
**Persecution** ill-treatment because of religion etc.
**Prejudice** unjustified dislike, often based on race or religion
**Scapegoat** person made to take blame for others

## Test yourself

What's persecution?

What's prejudice?

What's a scapegoat?

## Things to do

1 Explain what the Nazis were hoping to do by taking away the Jews' rights.

2 Give some reasons why their history and customs are so important to Jews.

3 Read the quotation from Pastor Niemoller. What lesson do you think it is trying to teach?

4 What sort of prejudice do you think happens in the world today? Why do you think it happens? Can individual people do anything about it?

5 Anne Frank was a Jewish girl whose family went into hiding from the Nazis in Holland. See if you can find a copy of *The Diary of Anne Frank* in your school or local library. Find out more about her life.

# Modern Jewish history

This section tells you about recent Jewish history.

The Jews 'home-land' is called Israel. Israel is a Hebrew word which means 'fighter for God'. Israel includes more or less the same area of land as Canaan, the country which Jews believe God gave to Abraham.

After World War II, many people in the world felt that Jews should have a country where they would be safe from persecution. Many Jews had gone to live there, and many more were **refugees** who wanted to go there. Israel was finally made a separate country in 1948. The law of Israel says that any Jew has the right to go and live there if they wish.

The Arab countries which are Israel's neighbours were very angry that the land had been given to the Jews. Arabs had lived there for hundreds of years, and they felt that the land should stay Arab. Jews feel that the land is theirs, because God promised it to Abraham and Jews lived there long before the first Arab settled there.

*The Western wall is an important place of pilgrimage*

*The position of Israel*

Soon after Israel became a separate country, Arab armies attacked it because their leaders thought that the state should not be allowed to exist. There were major wars between Jews and Arabs in 1956, 1967 and 1973. Although there have been suggestions for solving the disagreements, none has been accepted by all sides. This is the reason for much of the trouble in the Middle East today. There are still many problems along the borders of Israel, as countries fight over areas of land which they both claim should belong to them.

One reason why there is so much bitterness is that the area is very important for religious reasons. Jews, Christians and **Muslims** all have important events in their religious history which took place in Jerusalem, the capital city. This has been fought over for hundreds of years. It has now been divided. In 1967, Jews captured East Jerusalem, which includes the site of the Temple. The Temple was the holiest place in the Jewish religion. It was destroyed by the Romans in 70 CE. All that remains today is the Western Wall. This is an important place of **pilgrimage** for Jews, who go there to pray.

*This model shows what the Temple in Jerusalem looked like*

## New words

**Muslim** follower of the religion of Islam

**Pilgrimage** journey made for religious reasons

**Refugee** person who has no nationality

## Test yourself

What's a refugee?

What's the capital of Israel?

What remains of the Temple?

What's a pilgrimage?

## Things to do

1 What does the name 'Israel' mean? Why do you think Jews chose this name for their new country?

2 Why do you think that the law of Israel says that any Jew who wishes to can go to live there?

3 Explain why there are so many disagreements between Jews and Arabs about who the land of Israel should belong to.

4 Find out more about the Temple. When was it built? Why was it destroyed? Why is it still so important for Jews? (**Hint**: Looking up 'Jewish Temple', 'Jerusalem' and 'Judaism' in encyclopaedias would be a good way to start.)

# Judaism today

This section tells you about Jewish groups in the world today.

All followers of all religions are individual men and women, and of course they do not all have exactly the same ideas about their beliefs. Some people may think that one part of the religion is more important than another, and so on. Followers of Judaism all share belief in its basic teachings, but different groups of Jews do not agree about other parts of the religion and about how they should live their lives.

The main groups of Jews in the world today are Orthodox Jews, Reform Jews and Liberal Jews. More Jews are Orthodox than Reform or Liberal – over 75 per cent of Jews living in the UK today are Orthodox, although not all of them are 'strict' Orthodox.

*Orthodox Jews studying the scriptures*

## Orthodox Jews

Orthodox Jews believe that traditional ways of observing their religion are important. They keep the traditional laws of Judaism more strictly than other Jews. They believe that the Torah is the word of God, and shows how God wants people to live. The Torah will never

*Inside a Reform synagogue*

change although, as times change, the teachings may be applied in different ways, so that people can know what God wants whenever and wherever they live.

## Reform and Liberal Jews

Reform and Liberal Jews are not the same, but they share the belief that Judaism can change to fit different circumstances. The changes usually make it easier to live among people who are not Jews. For example, Reform and Liberal Jews do not keep the laws of the Torah as strictly as Orthodox Jews. They believe that laws can be changed or forgotten if they no longer seem to be useful. Orthodox Jews do not agree with these teachings.

## In the synagogue

In an Orthodox synagogue, men and women sit separately. In Reform and Liberal synagogues, they sit together, and men do not always wear a Kippah. In Orthodox services,

women do not take part except as members of the **congregation**. In Reform synagogues, women also take part in leading the services, and may become rabbis.

In Orthodox synagogues, the services are always held in Hebrew, although prayer books also have the prayers printed in English. In Reform and Liberal synagogues, prayers are more likely to be said in English. Orthodox services on the Sabbath and at festivals do not use musical instruments, but Reform synagogues often use organs. The way in which Sabbath and festivals are observed is also different.

### New word

**Congregation** group of people meeting for worship

## Test yourself

What are the main groups of Jews called?

What's a congregation?

What's a rabbi?

## Things to do

1 Look at the photograph of a Reform synagogue. Compare it with the photograph on page 8, which is of an Orthodox synagogue. What things can you see which are the same? What things can you see which are different?

2 What reasons can you give why Orthodox Jews think that men and women should sit separately for worship?

3 Reform Jews were given this name because they 're-formed' the traditional teaching of Judaism. Why do you think this happened?

4 Find out as much as you can about services in an Orthodox or a Reform synagogue. If you know someone who is Jewish, you could ask them, or try to find information in a library. Write an article describing what you have found out.

# Judaism in the home

This section tells you something about how Jews keep their religion at home.

Judaism is not just a set of beliefs, it is a way of life. The way in which Jews dress, eat and live are important parts of following their religion. This section looks at two of many different ways in which Jews carry out their beliefs at home.

## Mezuzahs

A **mezuzah** is a tiny scroll made of parchment. It has the prayer called the Shema written on it. The scroll is covered by a box which may be made of wood, plastic or metal. This is to protect the scroll. The box is fastened to the right-hand side of every doorpost, except doors to the bathroom and toilet. On their way in or out of the room, strict Jews touch the box. It reminds them that God is present in the house.

*A scribe writing a mezuzah scroll*

## Food

Judaism has laws about which foods may be eaten, and how food should be prepared. Strict Jews keep these laws very carefully. Most Jews keep at least some of the laws. Jewish food shops and more and more supermarkets sell food which has been manufactured so that it obeys Jewish food laws.

Food which Jews are allowed to eat is called **kosher**. All plants are kosher, but not all fish and animals are. The list of foods which are allowed is found in the book of Leviticus. Animals which chew the cud and have hooves which are split (for example cows and sheep) are kosher. Animals which do not (for example pigs and rabbits) are not kosher. Fish are allowed if they have fins and scales, but shellfish are not. Any animal which is to be eaten must be killed in a special way. Before being cooked, the meat is soaked in cold water and sprinkled with salt. This removes all the blood from it. A kosher butcher may prepare the meat so that it is ready to be cooked.

*A mezuzah*

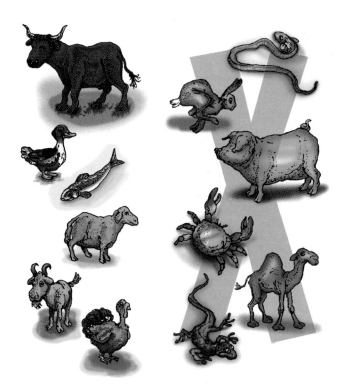

*The foods on the left are kosher, those on the right are not*

The laws say that meat and dairy foods cannot be eaten together, so for example, butter will not be used in a meat sandwich, nor will milk or cream sauces be eaten with meat.

Jews usually wait at least three hours before 'mixing' meat and milk, so a pudding with custard or cream, or coffee with milk, would not follow a meat course. To keep meat and milk totally separate, many Jewish kitchens have two sets of crockery, cutlery and tea-cloths. They also have two sinks or two bowls, so that the two sets can be washed separately.

For Jews, preparing food carefully and eating it are ways of worshipping God, because God has given the food. For the same reason, they thank him before and after meals.

## New words

**kosher** 'fit' – food which Jews can eat
**mezuzah** tiny scroll of the Shema

## Test yourself

What's a mezuzah?

What does kosher mean?

What is removed from kosher meat?

## Things to do

1 Using information in this section and in other sections you have read, describe as many ways as you can in which Jews follow their religion at home.

2 Look at the picture of the mezuzah. Explain why Jews have this scroll on their doors.

3 What reasons would a Jew give for obeying the laws about food?

4 Imagine you are inviting some Jewish friends for a meal. You can buy kosher food, but you need to plan a menu which would be suitable. What would you serve?

5 Find out more about which foods are kosher and which are not. Do some drawings to illustrate what you have found. (The Book of Leviticus, chapter 11, will help.)

# Special occasions I

This section tells you about the special things which happen to Jewish children.

## Babies

Jewish babies are always given a special Hebrew name, which is often chosen to remember a relation. This name is used as well as their 'ordinary' name, and it will always be used at important religious ceremonies.

## Circumcision

Healthy Jewish baby boys are **circumcised** on the eighth day after birth. (If a baby is ill, he will not be circumcised until he is well.) Circumcision means removing the foreskin, the flap of skin at the end of the penis. It is quite a common operation. Circumcision may be done by a doctor, or by a rabbi who is specially trained. A boy is given his name during this ceremony, which often takes place after morning prayers at the synagogue. Baby girls are given their names in the synagogue on the Sabbath after their birth.

## Bar Mitzvah

A Jewish boy becomes Bar Mitzvah at the age of thirteen. Bar Mitzvah means 'son of the commandments'. On the Sabbath after his thirteenth birthday, a boy recites the blessing on the Torah before it is read in the synagogue.

*A Bar Mitzvah ceremony in a synagogue in Jerusalem*

*This Bat Mitzvah girl is holding a copy of the Scriptures which she has decorated*

Some boys may read the passage from the Torah, too. He must have practised the Hebrew well enough to be able to read it in public. Friends and relatives will often come to the service, and there may be a celebration meal afterwards.

Once he has reached the age of Bar Mitzvah, a Jewish boy is counted as a man. He can be one of the ten men necessary before a synagogue service can be held, and he is expected to obey all the Jewish laws.

## Bat Mitzvah

A girl becomes Bat Mitzvah automatically at the age of twelve. Bat Mitzvah means 'daughter of the commandments'. Not all Orthodox synagogues have special services to celebrate Bat Mitzvahs. If they do, they are held on a Sunday rather than the Sabbath. Girls do not read from the Torah in an Orthodox synagogue. In a Reform synagogue, there is no difference between the services held for boys and girls. A party for family and friends is usually held after the service.

## New word

**Circumcision** removal of the foreskin

## Test yourself

What's circumcision?

What does Bar Mitzvah mean?

What does Bat Mitzvah mean?

## Things to do

**1** Why do you think Jewish babies are always given a Hebrew name?

**2** Why do you think Jewish boys and girls are called sons and daughters of the commandments when they become adult?

**3** How old do you think someone should be before they are counted as adult?

**4** Imagine you are a Jewish boy or girl at Bar or Bat Mitzvah. Write about your feelings.

**5** All names have meanings. Find out what your name means. Was there any special reason why you were given this name?

# Special occasions II

This section tells you about what happens at special events in a Jew's life.

## Marriage

Jews have always thought that it is important to be married. Usually, a Jew is expected to marry a Jew, because it is thought that it will be difficult to have a happy life with someone who does not understand and share their faith. A Jewish wedding service is conducted by a rabbi. Most take place in the synagogue, although they can be held in other places. Wherever the service is held, the bride and groom always stand under a special canopy. This is called a **huppah**. It is a symbol of the home which the couple will share. It is often decorated with flowers.

The couple drink from a glass of wine which has had a blessing said over it. The marriage contract is read and signed by the bridegroom. This says that the husband will look after his wife. Then the bridegroom gives the bride a ring, which she wears on the forefinger of her right hand. At the end of the service, the groom crushes a glass under his foot. (It is wrapped for safety.) No one really knows where or why this custom began, but it reminds the couple that there will be bad things as well as good in their married life, and they must face

*The bride and groom stand under the huppah*

Jewish graves

them together. It is also a reminder that the Temple in Jerusalem – the holiest place for Jews – was destroyed.

## Divorce

Jews allow couples to divorce, but there are usually great efforts to save a marriage. Friends and relatives will do their best to help the couple to sort out their problems. If divorce cannot be avoided, the husband gives the wife a certificate of divorce. This is the only way a Jewish marriage can be ended. Jewish law then allows a person to remarry.

## Death

Jews believe that funerals should take place as soon as possible after someone has died. If possible, it should be within 24 hours. Funeral services are always very simple. Jews believe that there should be no difference between rich and poor, because death happens to everyone. Most Jews do not allow bodies to be **cremated**, because they think that it destroys what God has made.

## After death

Jews do believe in a life after death, but it is not a very important part of their faith. They believe that it is more important to concentrate on this life, rather than think about what might happen in a future life.

## New words

**Cremation** burning a body after death
**Huppah** canopy used for wedding ceremony

## Test yourself

What's a huppah?

What does breaking the glass symbolize?

What's cremation?

## Things to do

1 Explain why a Jewish couple who are getting married stand under a huppah. Use the picture to help you describe what it is like.

2 What reasons can you think of why a Jew may prefer to marry a Jew?

3 Explain why Jews think that funerals should be as simple as possible.

4 Design a card which you could send to a Jewish couple for their wedding. (Try to find out the Hebrew greeting for the inside.)

5 Do you think there is a life after death? What might it be like if there is?

# Glossary

**Adonai** name for God (means Lord)
**Adultery** sexual relationship outside marriage
**Ark** cupboard which contains the scrolls
**Atonement** making up for something you have done wrong

**Bimah** platform on which the reading desk stands

**Challah bread** special bread for the Sabbath
**Christian** follower of Jesus
**Circumcision** removal of the foreskin
**Congregation** group of people meeting for worship
**Covenant** solemn agreement
**Covet** be jealous of what someone else owns
**Cremation** burning a body after death

**Dreidle** four-sided top

**Eternal** lasting for ever

**Fast** go without food and drink, often for religious reasons

**Greggor** rattle used by children at Purim

**Hagadah** book in which the Seder is written
**Hanukiah** candlestick with eight branches
**Havdalah** blessing which ends the Sabbath
**Hebrew** Jewish language
**Huppah** canopy used for wedding ceremony

**Idol** false god (often a statue)

**Judaism** Jewish religion

**Kiddush** blessing which begins the Sabbath
**Kippah** skull cap
**Kosher** 'fit' – food which Jews can eat

**Leaven** yeast, baking powder etc.

**Matzot** unleavened bread
**Mantle** cover for scrolls
**Menorah** seven-branched candlestick
**Mezuzah** tiny scroll of the Shema
**Miracle** event which cannot be explained
**Muslim** follower of the religion of Islam

**Nomad** person with no fixed home

**Parchment** writing surface made from animal skin
**Persecution** ill-treatment because of religion etc.
**Pharaoh** king of Egypt
**Pilgrimage** journey made for religious reasons
**Plague** disaster sent by God
**Prejudice** unjustified dislike, often based on race or religion
**Prophet** someone who tells people what God wants
**Psalm** sort of poem, used like a hymn

**Rabbi** Jewish teacher
**Refugee** person who has no nationality

**Sacrifice** offering made to a god
**Scapegoat** person made to take blame for others
**Scriptures** holy books
**Scroll** roll of parchment on which the Torah is written
**Seder** special Passover meal
**Sermon** special talk which teaches about religion
**Shabbat** Jewish holy day
**Shema** Jewish prayer
**Shofar** ram's horn instrument
**Sukkah** Hebrew word for tabernacle
**Synagogue** Jewish place of worship
**Symbol** something which has a special meaning, or stands for something else

**Tabernacle** sort of hut
**Tallit** prayer robe
**Talmud** collected teachings of the rabbis
**Tefillin** small leather boxes containing quotes from the Scriptures
**Temple** most important place of Jewish worship (destroyed 70 CE)
**Tenakh** Jewish Scriptures
**Torah** Books of Teaching

**Wilderness** place where little grows